FRANCE

By Ashley MacEachern

Illustrated by Michelle Barbera

Have you heard about **LANCE ARMSTRONG**—

the *bravest, strongest, toughest,* and *fastest* bike rider ever?

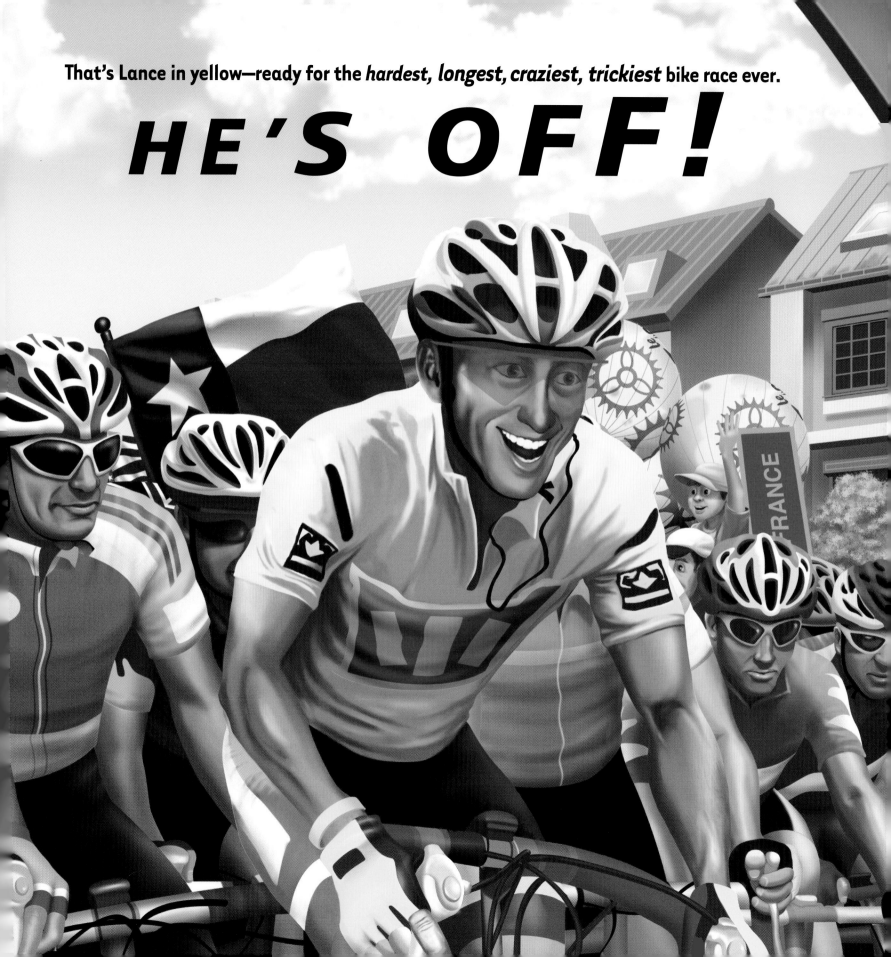

That's Lance in yellow—ready for the *hardest, longest, craziest, trickiest* bike race ever.

HE'S OFF!

Dark clouds thunder and rain pours down.
Lance gets soaked—but he doesn't complain.
He just pedals. . . .

Across fields of flowers comes a bumblebee swarm.

They buzzZZ and dive down low.

Lance gets stung! But he is brave.

He just pedals . . .

faster.

On the side of the road people cheer Lance on.
One fan gets in the way! Lance swerves and
crashes but gets back up.

He just pedals . . .
faster.

They race by the beach and the salty sea.

The tide comes in too high.

Lance splashes and slides—but he never stops.

He just pedals . . . *faster.*

Lance has an aching tummy and a woozy head.
He's sick, he's sore, but he won't lose hope. . . .
He just pedals . . . faster.

Around a bend they find a surprise:
a herd of cows blocking the way.
All the riders have to stop. Not Lance!

He just pedals . . .

faster.

Back and forth they **z o o m** down a mountain.

Watch out, there's a big crash ahead!

Lance rides off the road! Hang on!

He just pedals . . .

and pedals . . .

faster.

Mange tes Légumes

He hits a sharp rock—pop! His tire is flat!

Lance fixes it, lickety-split.
With no time to lose, he gets
back on his bike.

He just pedals . . .

faster.

Can you tell by now? Lance never quits!

When the race gets tough, he doesn't give up.

Instead, *he just pedals . . .*

faster and *faster*

When I was a little boy, I loved to ride my bike.

But if someone had told me then that I would grow up
to win the biggest bike race in the world—
the Tour de France—
seven times in a row,
I would have said they were crazy.

I didn't even know where France was!

The Tour de France is more than one hundred years old.
It takes three weeks to ride and covers more than 2,000 miles.
Some people call the Tour the greatest
(and hardest) sports event in the world.

I agree: There is nothing else like it.
But the race is about more than sports to me.

For me the Tour is about dreams coming true and the power of
believing in yourself to do the impossible.

What is your dream?

What is your Tour de France?

Find out what you are good at and love to do.

Go for it and never quit.

Just like in life, at the Tour de France anything can happen. In fact, every situation described by Ashley MacEachern in this book has happened at one time or another throughout the history of the Tour. Here's a listing, in the order of Michelle Barbera's fantastic illustrations.

- Rain is common every year. Lance uses it to his advantage.
- In the first week of the 2005 Tour, Lance was stung by a bee.
- Lance crashed in 2003 when his handlebars snagged a bystander's backpack.
- Lance avoided a massive crash on the slick Passage du Gois (passable only at low tide) in 1999, helping him achieve his first Tour win.
- Lance began the 2004 Tour with a stomach virus, but he kept going.
- The Tour de France is an open course, so every year all sorts of things can and do get in the way. Lance never *jumped* over a herd of cows, but Tour de France cyclists have been slowed over the years by trains, photographers, fans, cars, and animals of all shapes and sizes—including cows.
- In 2003, Lance decided to veer off the road to avoid hitting Joseba Beloki, who had crashed in front of him.
- Flat tires are a reality and a risk every year. Team cars provide support.
- Between 1999 and 2005, Lance won seven consecutive Tours, setting the world record.

Have fun looking for recurring characters! Can you find the lady with the poodle (five times), El Diablo (seven times), the man with the bulldog (three times), and the French reporter (four times)? Try to spot this fan from Texas (one time).

MORE ABOUT LANCE

Lance Armstrong began riding his bike when he was five years old. At thirteen, he won the Iron Kids triathlon. He began his professional cycling career at sixteen. Over the next decade, he won numerous national and international titles, including multiple stage victories at the Tour de France. Then, when he was only twenty-five, he was diagnosed with cancer. Lance was given less than a 50 percent chance of survival. Many doubted he would live, let alone race again.

But he beat cancer and returned to cycling to win seven consecutive Tour de France races from 1999 through 2005. The Tour de France is arguably the most difficult sporting event in the world. It lasts twenty-one days and covers more than 2,000 miles. But as difficult as it is, Lance has always said that fighting cancer was harder. Because of this, he has great respect for the cancer community—all the millions of patients and survivors, friends and families who struggle with cancer every day. He rode and won for them, to show the world that anything is possible. To show the world there is always hope. To encourage people to never give up.

In 1997 he started the Lance Armstrong Foundation. The LAF funds cancer research and provides programs for survivorship. In the summer of 2004, to celebrate Lance's inspirational defeat of cancer and unprecedented athletic achievements, Nike created the yellow LIVESTRONG wristbands for the foundation. More than 60 million wristbands have been sold, and all of the profits go to the LAF. Lance and his yellow wristbands have become a global symbol of hope and living strong.

A portion of the proceeds from this book will be donated to the LAF.

Collins is an imprint of HarperCollins Publishers.

LANCE IN FRANCE

Text copyright © 2008 by Ashley MacEachern   Illustrations copyright © 2008 by Michelle Barbera
Manufactured in China. All rights reserved. No part of this book may be used or reproduced in any manner whatsoever without written permission except in the case of brief quotations embodied in critical articles and reviews. For information address HarperCollins Children's Books, a division of HarperCollins Publishers, 1350 Avenue of the Americas, New York, NY 10019.   www.harpercollinschildrens.com   Library of Congress Cataloging-in-Publication Data MacEachern, Ashley.   Lance in France / by Ashley MacEachern ; illustrated by Michelle Barbera.— 1st ed.   p.   cm.
ISBN 978-0-06-113192-9 (trade bdg.) — ISBN 978-0-06-113193-6 (lib. bdg.)   1. Armstrong, Lance—Juvenile literature.   2. Tour de France (Bicycle race)—Juvenile literature.   3. Cyclists—United States—Conduct of life—Juvenile literature.   I. Barbera, Michelle, ill.   II. Title.   GV1051.A76M33 2008
796.6'2092—dc22   [B]   2007010876   Designed by Stephanie Bart-Horvath   1 2 3 4 5 6 7 8 9 10   ❖   First Edition